T0023728

MUSHROOM
LOGBOOK

BELONGS TO:

_____

IF FOUND, REACH ME AT:

_____

_____

LOCATION _____ **DATE** _____

_____

_____

_____

GPS COORDINATES _____

WEATHER _____

HABITAT (Note where mushroom is sprouting—e.g., in disturbed soil, on decomposing log, at base of tree trunk—

and identify nearby trees and plants.) _____

_____

_____

_____

_____

PROBABLE SPECIES _____

CAP CHARACTERISTICS

Color _____	Spore color _____
Shape _____	Diameter _____
Texture _____	
Condition _____	
Gills, teeth, pores, or other _____	
Additional notes (e.g., odor) _____	

_____

_____

STEM CHARACTERISTICS

Color _____	Height _____
Shape _____	Diameter _____
Texture _____	
Additional notes (e.g., stem base details) _____	

_____

_____

_____

LOCATION

GPS COORDINATES

WEATHER

HABITAT (Note where mushroom is sprouting—e.g., in disturbed soil, on decomposing log, at base of tree trunk—and identify nearby trees and plants.)

PROBABLE SPECIES

CAP CHARACTERISTICS

Color   Spore color

Shape   Diameter

Texture

Condition

Gills, teeth, pores, or other

Additional notes (e.g., odor)

STEM CHARACTERISTICS

Color   Height

Shape   Diameter

Texture

Additional notes (e.g., stem base details)

LOCATION _____ DATE _____

_____

_____

GPS COORDINATES _____

WEATHER _____

HABITAT (Note where mushroom is sprouting—e.g., in disturbed soil, on decomposing log, at base of tree trunk—

and identify nearby trees and plants.) _____

_____

_____

_____

_____

PROBABLE SPECIES _____

CAP CHARACTERISTICS

Color _____ Spore color _____

Shape _____ Diameter _____

Texture _____

Condition _____

Gills, teeth, pores, or other _____

Additional notes (e.g., odor) _____

_____

_____

STEM CHARACTERISTICS

Color _____ Height _____

Shape _____ Diameter _____

Texture _____

Additional notes (e.g., stem base details) _____

_____

_____

LOCATION

DATE

GPS COORDINATES

WEATHER

HABITAT (Note where mushroom is sprouting—e.g., in disturbed soil, on decomposing log, at base of tree trunk—and identify nearby trees and plants.)

PROBABLE SPECIES

CAP CHARACTERISTICS

Color

Spore color

Shape

Diameter

Texture

Condition

Gills, teeth, pores, or other

Additional notes (e.g., odor)

STEM CHARACTERISTICS

Color

Height

Shape

Diameter

Texture

Additional notes (e.g., stem base details)

LOCATION   **DATE**

GPS COORDINATES

WEATHER

HABITAT (Note where mushroom is sprouting—e.g., in disturbed soil, on decomposing log, at base of tree trunk—

and identify nearby trees and plants.)

PROBABLE SPECIES

CAP CHARACTERISTICS

Color   Spore color

Shape   Diameter

Texture

Condition

Gills, teeth, pores, or other

Additional notes (e.g., odor)

STEM CHARACTERISTICS

Color   Height

Shape   Diameter

Texture

Additional notes (e.g., stem base details)

LOCATION

DATE

GPS COORDINATES

WEATHER

HABITAT (Note where mushroom is sprouting—e.g., in disturbed soil, on decomposing log, at base of tree trunk—and identify nearby trees and plants.)

PROBABLE SPECIES

CAP CHARACTERISTICS

Color

Spore color

Shape

Diameter

Texture

Condition

Gills, teeth, pores, or other

Additional notes (e.g., odor)

STEM CHARACTERISTICS

Color

Height

Shape

Diameter

Texture

Additional notes (e.g., stem base details)

LOCATION _____ DATE _____

_____

_____

GPS COORDINATES _____

WEATHER _____

HABITAT (Note where mushroom is sprouting—e.g., in disturbed soil, on decomposing log, at base of tree trunk—

and identify nearby trees and plants.) _____

_____

_____

_____

_____

PROBABLE SPECIES _____

CAP CHARACTERISTICS

  Color _____   Spore color _____

  Shape _____   Diameter _____

  Texture _____

  Condition _____

  Gills, teeth, pores, or other _____

  Additional notes (e.g., odor) _____

_____

_____

_____

STEM CHARACTERISTICS

  Color _____   Height _____

  Shape _____   Diameter _____

  Texture _____

  Additional notes (e.g., stem base details) _____

_____

_____

_____

LOCATION

DATE

GPS COORDINATES

WEATHER

HABITAT (Note where mushroom is sprouting—e.g., in disturbed soil, on decomposing log, at base of tree trunk—
and identify nearby trees and plants.)

PROBABLE SPECIES

CAP CHARACTERISTICS

Color

Spore color

Shape

Diameter

Texture

Condition

Gills, teeth, pores, or other

Additional notes (e.g., odor)

STEM CHARACTERISTICS

Color

Height

Shape

Diameter

Texture

Additional notes (e.g., stem base details)

LOCATION

DATE

GPS COORDINATES

WEATHER

HABITAT (Note where mushroom is sprouting—e.g., in disturbed soil, on decomposing log, at base of tree trunk—and identify nearby trees and plants.)

PROBABLE SPECIES

CAP CHARACTERISTICS

Color   Spore color

Shape   Diameter

Texture

Condition

Gills, teeth, pores, or other

Additional notes (e.g., odor)

STEM CHARACTERISTICS

Color   Height

Shape   Diameter

Texture

Additional notes (e.g., stem base details)

LOCATION

DATE

GPS COORDINATES

WEATHER

HABITAT (Note where mushroom is sprouting—e.g., in disturbed soil, on decomposing log, at base of tree trunk—and identify nearby trees and plants.)

PROBABLE SPECIES

CAP CHARACTERISTICS

Color   Spore color

Shape   Diameter

Texture

Condition

Gills, teeth, pores, or other

Additional notes (e.g., odor)

STEM CHARACTERISTICS

Color   Height

Shape   Diameter

Texture

Additional notes (e.g., stem base details)

LOCATION   DATE

GPS COORDINATES

WEATHER

HABITAT (Note where mushroom is sprouting—e.g., in disturbed soil, on decomposing log, at base of tree trunk—
and identify nearby trees and plants.)

PROBABLE SPECIES

CAP CHARACTERISTICS

Color   Spore color

Shape   Diameter

Texture

Condition

Gills, teeth, pores, or other

Additional notes (e.g., odor)

STEM CHARACTERISTICS

Color   Height

Shape   Diameter

Texture

Additional notes (e.g., stem base details)

LOCATION   DATE

GPS COORDINATES

WEATHER

HABITAT (Note where mushroom is sprouting—e.g., in disturbed soil, on decomposing log, at base of tree trunk—

and identify nearby trees and plants.)

PROBABLE SPECIES

CAP CHARACTERISTICS

Color   Spore color

Shape   Diameter

Texture

Condition

Gills, teeth, pores, or other

Additional notes (e.g., odor)

STEM CHARACTERISTICS

Color   Height

Shape   Diameter

Texture

Additional notes (e.g., stem base details)

LOCATION

DATE

GPS COORDINATES

WEATHER

HABITAT (Note where mushroom is sprouting—e.g., in disturbed soil, on decomposing log, at base of tree trunk—and identify nearby trees and plants.)

PROBABLE SPECIES

CAP CHARACTERISTICS

Color

Spore color

Shape

Diameter

Texture

Condition

Gills, teeth, pores, or other

Additional notes (e.g., odor)

STEM CHARACTERISTICS

Color

Height

Shape

Diameter

Texture

Additional notes (e.g., stem base details)

LOCATION _____ DATE _____

_____

_____

GPS COORDINATES _____

WEATHER _____

HABITAT (Note where mushroom is sprouting—e.g., in disturbed soil, on decomposing log, at base of tree trunk—

and identify nearby trees and plants.) _____

_____

_____

_____

_____

PROBABLE SPECIES _____

CAP CHARACTERISTICS

    Color _____   Spore color _____

    Shape _____   Diameter _____

    Texture _____

    Condition _____

    Gills, teeth, pores, or other _____

    Additional notes (e.g., odor) _____

_____

_____

STEM CHARACTERISTICS

    Color _____   Height _____

    Shape _____   Diameter _____

    Texture _____

    Additional notes (e.g., stem base details) _____

_____

_____

LOCATION   DATE

_____

_____

_____

GPS COORDINATES

_____

WEATHER

_____

HABITAT (Note where mushroom is sprouting—e.g., in disturbed soil, on decomposing log, at base of tree trunk—

and identify nearby trees and plants.)

_____

_____

_____

_____

PROBABLE SPECIES

CAP CHARACTERISTICS

Color	Spore color
Shape	Diameter
Texture	
Condition	
Gills, teeth, pores, or other	
Additional notes (e.g., odor)	

_____

_____

STEM CHARACTERISTICS

Color	Height
Shape	Diameter
Texture	
Additional notes (e.g., stem base details)	

_____

_____

_____

LOCATION

DATE

GPS COORDINATES

WEATHER

HABITAT (Note where mushroom is sprouting—e.g., in disturbed soil, on decomposing log, at base of tree trunk—and identify nearby trees and plants.)

PROBABLE SPECIES

CAP CHARACTERISTICS

Color

Spore color

Shape

Diameter

Texture

Condition

Gills, teeth, pores, or other

Additional notes (e.g., odor)

STEM CHARACTERISTICS

Color

Height

Shape

Diameter

Texture

Additional notes (e.g., stem base details)

LOCATION   DATE

_____   _____

_____

_____

GPS COORDINATES
_____

WEATHER
_____

HABITAT (Note where mushroom is sprouting—e.g., in disturbed soil, on decomposing log, at base of tree trunk—

and identify nearby trees and plants.)
_____

_____

_____

_____

_____

PROBABLE SPECIES
_____

CAP CHARACTERISTICS
_____

    Color _____   Spore color _____

    Shape _____   Diameter _____

    Texture _____

    Condition _____

    Gills, teeth, pores, or other _____

    Additional notes (e.g., odor) _____

_____

_____

_____

STEM CHARACTERISTICS
_____

    Color _____   Height _____

    Shape _____   Diameter _____

    Texture _____

    Additional notes (e.g., stem base details) _____

_____

_____

_____

LOCATION   DATE

GPS COORDINATES

WEATHER

HABITAT (Note where mushroom is sprouting—e.g., in disturbed soil, on decomposing log, at base of tree trunk—

and identify nearby trees and plants.)

PROBABLE SPECIES

CAP CHARACTERISTICS

    Color   Spore color

    Shape   Diameter

    Texture

    Condition

    Gills, teeth, pores, or other

    Additional notes (e.g., odor)

STEM CHARACTERISTICS

    Color   Height

    Shape   Diameter

    Texture

    Additional notes (e.g., stem base details)

LOCATION   DATE

GPS COORDINATES

WEATHER

HABITAT (Note where mushroom is sprouting—e.g., in disturbed soil, on decomposing log, at base of tree trunk—

and identify nearby trees and plants.)

PROBABLE SPECIES

CAP CHARACTERISTICS

Color	Spore color
Shape	Diameter
Texture	
Condition	
Gills, teeth, pores, or other	
Additional notes (e.g., odor)	

STEM CHARACTERISTICS

Color	Height
Shape	Diameter
Texture	
Additional notes (e.g., stem base details)	

LOCATION   DATE

_____

_____

GPS COORDINATES
_____

WEATHER
_____

HABITAT (Note where mushroom is sprouting—e.g., in disturbed soil, on decomposing log, at base of tree trunk—

and identify nearby trees and plants.)
_____

_____

_____

_____

PROBABLE SPECIES
_____

CAP CHARACTERISTICS

Color   Spore color

Shape   Diameter

Texture

Condition

Gills, teeth, pores, or other

Additional notes (e.g., odor)

_____

_____

STEM CHARACTERISTICS

Color   Height

Shape   Diameter

Texture

Additional notes (e.g., stem base details)

_____

_____

LOCATION   DATE

GPS COORDINATES

WEATHER

HABITAT (Note where mushroom is sprouting—e.g., in disturbed soil, on decomposing log, at base of tree trunk—and identify nearby trees and plants.)

PROBABLE SPECIES

CAP CHARACTERISTICS

Color   Spore color

Shape   Diameter

Texture

Condition

Gills, teeth, pores, or other

Additional notes (e.g., odor)

STEM CHARACTERISTICS

Color   Height

Shape   Diameter

Texture

Additional notes (e.g., stem base details)

LOCATION   DATE

GPS COORDINATES

WEATHER

HABITAT (Note where mushroom is sprouting—e.g., in disturbed soil, on decomposing log, at base of tree trunk—
and identify nearby trees and plants.)

PROBABLE SPECIES

CAP CHARACTERISTICS

Color   Spore color

Shape   Diameter

Texture

Condition

Gills, teeth, pores, or other

Additional notes (e.g., odor)

STEM CHARACTERISTICS

Color   Height

Shape   Diameter

Texture

Additional notes (e.g., stem base details)

LOCATION

DATE

GPS COORDINATES

WEATHER

HABITAT (Note where mushroom is sprouting—e.g., in disturbed soil, on decomposing log, at base of tree trunk—and identify nearby trees and plants.)

PROBABLE SPECIES

CAP CHARACTERISTICS

Color   Spore color

Shape   Diameter

Texture

Condition

Gills, teeth, pores, or other

Additional notes (e.g., odor)

STEM CHARACTERISTICS

Color   Height

Shape   Diameter

Texture

Additional notes (e.g., stem base details)

LOCATION

DATE

GPS COORDINATES

WEATHER

HABITAT (Note where mushroom is sprouting—e.g., in disturbed soil, on decomposing log, at base of tree trunk—

and identify nearby trees and plants.)

PROBABLE SPECIES

CAP CHARACTERISTICS

Color

Spore color

Shape

Diameter

Texture

Condition

Gills, teeth, pores, or other

Additional notes (e.g., odor)

STEM CHARACTERISTICS

Color

Height

Shape

Diameter

Texture

Additional notes (e.g., stem base details)

LOCATION _____ **DATE** _____

_____

_____

_____

GPS COORDINATES _____

WEATHER _____

HABITAT (Note where mushroom is sprouting—e.g., in disturbed soil, on decomposing log, at base of tree trunk—

and identify nearby trees and plants.) _____

_____

_____

_____

_____

PROBABLE SPECIES _____

CAP CHARACTERISTICS

Color	Spore color
Shape	Diameter
Texture	
Condition	
Gills, teeth, pores, or other	
Additional notes (e.g., odor)	

STEM CHARACTERISTICS

Color	Height
Shape	Diameter
Texture	
Additional notes (e.g., stem base details)	

LOCATION _____   DATE _____

_____

_____

GPS COORDINATES _____

WEATHER _____

HABITAT (Note where mushroom is sprouting—e.g., in disturbed soil, on decomposing log, at base of tree trunk—

and identify nearby trees and plants.) _____

_____

_____

_____

_____

PROBABLE SPECIES _____

CAP CHARACTERISTICS _____

   Color _____   Spore color _____

   Shape _____   Diameter _____

   Texture _____

   Condition _____

   Gills, teeth, pores, or other _____

   Additional notes (e.g., odor) _____

_____

_____

_____

STEM CHARACTERISTICS _____

   Color _____   Height _____

   Shape _____   Diameter _____

   Texture _____

   Additional notes (e.g., stem base details) _____

_____

_____

_____

_____

LOCATION   DATE

GPS COORDINATES

WEATHER

HABITAT (Note where mushroom is sprouting—e.g., in disturbed soil, on decomposing log, at base of tree trunk—

and identify nearby trees and plants.)

PROBABLE SPECIES

CAP CHARACTERISTICS

Color	Spore color
Shape	Diameter
Texture	
Condition	
Gills, teeth, pores, or other	
Additional notes (e.g., odor)	

STEM CHARACTERISTICS

Color	Height
Shape	Diameter
Texture	
Additional notes (e.g., stem base details)	

LOCATION _____ DATE _____

_____

_____

GPS COORDINATES _____

WEATHER _____

HABITAT (Note where mushroom is sprouting—e.g., in disturbed soil, on decomposing log, at base of tree trunk—

and identify nearby trees and plants.) _____

_____

_____

_____

_____

PROBABLE SPECIES _____

CAP CHARACTERISTICS

   Color _____ Spore color _____

   Shape _____ Diameter _____

   Texture _____

   Condition _____

   Gills, teeth, pores, or other _____

   Additional notes (e.g., odor) _____

_____

_____

STEM CHARACTERISTICS

   Color _____ Height _____

   Shape _____ Diameter _____

   Texture _____

   Additional notes (e.g., stem base details) _____

_____

_____

_____

LOCATION   DATE

GPS COORDINATES

WEATHER

HABITAT (Note where mushroom is sprouting—e.g., in disturbed soil, on decomposing log, at base of tree trunk—
and identify nearby trees and plants.)

PROBABLE SPECIES

CAP CHARACTERISTICS

Color   Spore color

Shape   Diameter

Texture

Condition

Gills, teeth, pores, or other

Additional notes (e.g., odor)

STEM CHARACTERISTICS

Color   Height

Shape   Diameter

Texture

Additional notes (e.g., stem base details)

LOCATION

DATE

GPS COORDINATES

WEATHER

HABITAT (Note where mushroom is sprouting—e.g., in disturbed soil, on decomposing log, at base of tree trunk—
and identify nearby trees and plants.)

PROBABLE SPECIES

CAP CHARACTERISTICS

Color	Spore color
Shape	Diameter
Texture	
Condition	
Gills, teeth, pores, or other	
Additional notes (e.g., odor)	

STEM CHARACTERISTICS

Color	Height
Shape	Diameter
Texture	
Additional notes (e.g., stem base details)	

LOCATION _____ DATE _____

_____

_____

GPS COORDINATES _____

WEATHER _____

HABITAT (Note where mushroom is sprouting—e.g., in disturbed soil, on decomposing log, at base of tree trunk—

and identify nearby trees and plants.) _____

_____

_____

_____

_____

PROBABLE SPECIES _____

CAP CHARACTERISTICS

Color	Spore color
Shape	Diameter
Texture	
Condition	
Gills, teeth, pores, or other	
Additional notes (e.g., odor)	

STEM CHARACTERISTICS

Color	Height
Shape	Diameter
Texture	
Additional notes (e.g., stem base details)	

LOCATION   DATE

GPS COORDINATES

WEATHER

HABITAT (Note where mushroom is sprouting—e.g., in disturbed soil, on decomposing log, at base of tree trunk—

and identify nearby trees and plants.)

PROBABLE SPECIES

CAP CHARACTERISTICS

Color   Spore color

Shape   Diameter

Texture

Condition

Gills, teeth, pores, or other

Additional notes (e.g., odor)

STEM CHARACTERISTICS

Color   Height

Shape   Diameter

Texture

Additional notes (e.g., stem base details)

LOCATION

DATE

GPS COORDINATES

WEATHER

HABITAT (Note where mushroom is sprouting—e.g., in disturbed soil, on decomposing log, at base of tree trunk—and identify nearby trees and plants.)

PROBABLE SPECIES

CAP CHARACTERISTICS

Color

Spore color

Shape

Diameter

Texture

Condition

Gills, teeth, pores, or other

Additional notes (e.g., odor)

STEM CHARACTERISTICS

Color

Height

Shape

Diameter

Texture

Additional notes (e.g., stem base details)

LOCATION   DATE

_____

_____

_____

GPS COORDINATES

WEATHER

HABITAT (Note where mushroom is sprouting—e.g., in disturbed soil, on decomposing log, at base of tree trunk—

and identify nearby trees and plants.)

_____

_____

_____

_____

PROBABLE SPECIES

CAP CHARACTERISTICS

Color	Spore color
Shape	Diameter
Texture	
Condition	
Gills, teeth, pores, or other	
Additional notes (e.g., odor)	

STEM CHARACTERISTICS

Color	Height
Shape	Diameter
Texture	
Additional notes (e.g., stem base details)	

LOCATION _____ DATE _____

_____

_____

GPS COORDINATES _____

WEATHER _____

HABITAT (Note where mushroom is sprouting—e.g., in disturbed soil, on decomposing log, at base of tree trunk—

and identify nearby trees and plants.) _____

_____

_____

_____

_____

PROBABLE SPECIES _____

CAP CHARACTERISTICS

    Color _____ Spore color _____

    Shape _____ Diameter _____

    Texture _____

    Condition _____

    Gills, teeth, pores, or other _____

    Additional notes (e.g., odor) _____

_____

_____

STEM CHARACTERISTICS

    Color _____ Height _____

    Shape _____ Diameter _____

    Texture _____

    Additional notes (e.g., stem base details) _____

_____

_____

LOCATION

DATE

GPS COORDINATES

WEATHER

HABITAT (Note where mushroom is sprouting—e.g., in disturbed soil, on decomposing log, at base of tree trunk—and identify nearby trees and plants.)

PROBABLE SPECIES

CAP CHARACTERISTICS

Color	Spore color
Shape	Diameter
Texture	
Condition	
Gills, teeth, pores, or other	
Additional notes (e.g., odor)	

STEM CHARACTERISTICS

Color	Height
Shape	Diameter
Texture	
Additional notes (e.g., stem base details)	

LOCATION   **DATE**

GPS COORDINATES

WEATHER

HABITAT (Note where mushroom is sprouting—e.g., in disturbed soil, on decomposing log, at base of tree trunk—

and identify nearby trees and plants.)

PROBABLE SPECIES

CAP CHARACTERISTICS

    Color   Spore color

    Shape   Diameter

    Texture

    Condition

    Gills, teeth, pores, or other

    Additional notes (e.g., odor)

STEM CHARACTERISTICS

    Color   Height

    Shape   Diameter

    Texture

    Additional notes (e.g., stem base details)

LOCATION   DATE

GPS COORDINATES

WEATHER

HABITAT (Note where mushroom is sprouting—e.g., in disturbed soil, on decomposing log, at base of tree trunk—

and identify nearby trees and plants.)

PROBABLE SPECIES

CAP CHARACTERISTICS

Color   Spore color

Shape   Diameter

Texture

Condition

Gills, teeth, pores, or other

Additional notes (e.g., odor)

STEM CHARACTERISTICS

Color   Height

Shape   Diameter

Texture

Additional notes (e.g., stem base details)

LOCATION

DATE

GPS COORDINATES

WEATHER

HABITAT (Note where mushroom is sprouting—e.g., in disturbed soil, on decomposing log, at base of tree trunk—

and identify nearby trees and plants.)

PROBABLE SPECIES

CAP CHARACTERISTICS

Color   Spore color

Shape   Diameter

Texture

Condition

Gills, teeth, pores, or other

Additional notes (e.g., odor)

STEM CHARACTERISTICS

Color   Height

Shape   Diameter

Texture

Additional notes (e.g., stem base details)

LOCATION   DATE

_____

_____

_____

GPS COORDINATES

WEATHER

HABITAT (Note where mushroom is sprouting—e.g., in disturbed soil, on decomposing log, at base of tree trunk—

and identify nearby trees and plants.)

_____

_____

_____

_____

_____

PROBABLE SPECIES

CAP CHARACTERISTICS

Color	Spore color
Shape	Diameter
Texture	
Condition	
Gills, teeth, pores, or other	
Additional notes (e.g., odor)	

STEM CHARACTERISTICS

Color	Height
Shape	Diameter
Texture	
Additional notes (e.g., stem base details)	

LOCATION   DATE

GPS COORDINATES

WEATHER

HABITAT (Note where mushroom is sprouting—e.g., in disturbed soil, on decomposing log, at base of tree trunk—

and identify nearby trees and plants.)

PROBABLE SPECIES

CAP CHARACTERISTICS

Color   Spore color

Shape   Diameter

Texture

Condition

Gills, teeth, pores, or other

Additional notes (e.g., odor)

STEM CHARACTERISTICS

Color   Height

Shape   Diameter

Texture

Additional notes (e.g., stem base details)

LOCATION   DATE

GPS COORDINATES

WEATHER

HABITAT (Note where mushroom is sprouting—e.g., in disturbed soil, on decomposing log, at base of tree trunk—

and identify nearby trees and plants.)

PROBABLE SPECIES

CAP CHARACTERISTICS

    Color   Spore color

    Shape   Diameter

    Texture

    Condition

    Gills, teeth, pores, or other

    Additional notes (e.g., odor)

STEM CHARACTERISTICS

    Color   Height

    Shape   Diameter

    Texture

    Additional notes (e.g., stem base details)

LOCATION   DATE

GPS COORDINATES

WEATHER

HABITAT (Note where mushroom is sprouting—e.g., in disturbed soil, on decomposing log, at base of tree trunk—
and identify nearby trees and plants.)

PROBABLE SPECIES

CAP CHARACTERISTICS

Color   Spore color

Shape   Diameter

Texture

Condition

Gills, teeth, pores, or other

Additional notes (e.g., odor)

STEM CHARACTERISTICS

Color   Height

Shape   Diameter

Texture

Additional notes (e.g., stem base details)

LOCATION											DATE

GPS COORDINATES

WEATHER

HABITAT (Note where mushroom is sprouting—e.g., in disturbed soil, on decomposing log, at base of tree trunk—and identify nearby trees and plants.)

PROBABLE SPECIES

CAP CHARACTERISTICS

Color									Spore color

Shape									Diameter

Texture

Condition

Gills, teeth, pores, or other

Additional notes (e.g., odor)

STEM CHARACTERISTICS

Color									Height

Shape									Diameter

Texture

Additional notes (e.g., stem base details)

LOCATION

DATE

GPS COORDINATES

WEATHER

HABITAT (Note where mushroom is sprouting—e.g., in disturbed soil, on decomposing log, at base of tree trunk—

and identify nearby trees and plants.)

PROBABLE SPECIES

CAP CHARACTERISTICS

Color   Spore color

Shape   Diameter

Texture

Condition

Gills, teeth, pores, or other

Additional notes (e.g., odor)

STEM CHARACTERISTICS

Color   Height

Shape   Diameter

Texture

Additional notes (e.g., stem base details)

LOCATION   DATE

GPS COORDINATES

WEATHER

HABITAT (Note where mushroom is sprouting—e.g., in disturbed soil, on decomposing log, at base of tree trunk—

and identify nearby trees and plants.)

PROBABLE SPECIES

CAP CHARACTERISTICS

Color   Spore color

Shape   Diameter

Texture

Condition

Gills, teeth, pores, or other

Additional notes (e.g., odor)

STEM CHARACTERISTICS

Color   Height

Shape   Diameter

Texture

Additional notes (e.g., stem base details)

LOCATION _____ DATE _____

_____

_____

GPS COORDINATES _____

WEATHER _____

HABITAT (Note where mushroom is sprouting—e.g., in disturbed soil, on decomposing log, at base of tree trunk—

and identify nearby trees and plants.) _____

_____

_____

_____

_____

PROBABLE SPECIES _____

CAP CHARACTERISTICS

Color _____ Spore color _____

Shape _____ Diameter _____

Texture _____

Condition _____

Gills, teeth, pores, or other _____

Additional notes (e.g., odor) _____

_____

_____

STEM CHARACTERISTICS

Color _____ Height _____

Shape _____ Diameter _____

Texture _____

Additional notes (e.g., stem base details) _____

_____

_____

_____

LOCATION   DATE

GPS COORDINATES

WEATHER

HABITAT (Note where mushroom is sprouting—e.g., in disturbed soil, on decomposing log, at base of tree trunk—

and identify nearby trees and plants.)

PROBABLE SPECIES

CAP CHARACTERISTICS

Color	Spore color
Shape	Diameter
Texture	
Condition	
Gills, teeth, pores, or other	
Additional notes (e.g., odor)	

STEM CHARACTERISTICS

Color	Height
Shape	Diameter
Texture	
Additional notes (e.g., stem base details)	

LOCATION   DATE

GPS COORDINATES

WEATHER

HABITAT (Note where mushroom is sprouting—e.g., in disturbed soil, on decomposing log, at base of tree trunk—and identify nearby trees and plants.)

PROBABLE SPECIES

CAP CHARACTERISTICS

Color	Spore color
Shape	Diameter
Texture	
Condition	
Gills, teeth, pores, or other	
Additional notes (e.g., odor)	

STEM CHARACTERISTICS

Color	Height
Shape	Diameter
Texture	
Additional notes (e.g., stem base details)	

LOCATION   DATE

_____

_____

_____

GPS COORDINATES
_____

WEATHER
_____

HABITAT (Note where mushroom is sprouting—e.g., in disturbed soil, on decomposing log, at base of tree trunk—

and identify nearby trees and plants.)
_____

_____

_____

_____

_____

PROBABLE SPECIES
_____

CAP CHARACTERISTICS
_____

    Color   Spore color
_____

    Shape   Diameter
_____

    Texture
_____

    Condition
_____

    Gills, teeth, pores, or other
_____

    Additional notes (e.g., odor)
_____

_____

_____

STEM CHARACTERISTICS
_____

    Color   Height
_____

    Shape   Diameter
_____

    Texture
_____

    Additional notes (e.g., stem base details)
_____

_____

_____

LOCATION

DATE

GPS COORDINATES

WEATHER

HABITAT (Note where mushroom is sprouting—e.g., in disturbed soil, on decomposing log, at base of tree trunk—

and identify nearby trees and plants.)

PROBABLE SPECIES

CAP CHARACTERISTICS

Color   Spore color

Shape   Diameter

Texture

Condition

Gills, teeth, pores, or other

Additional notes (e.g., odor)

STEM CHARACTERISTICS

Color   Height

Shape   Diameter

Texture

Additional notes (e.g., stem base details)

LOCATION

DATE

GPS COORDINATES

WEATHER

HABITAT (Note where mushroom is sprouting—e.g., in disturbed soil, on decomposing log, at base of tree trunk—
and identify nearby trees and plants.)

PROBABLE SPECIES

CAP CHARACTERISTICS

Color   Spore color

Shape   Diameter

Texture

Condition

Gills, teeth, pores, or other

Additional notes (e.g., odor)

STEM CHARACTERISTICS

Color   Height

Shape   Diameter

Texture

Additional notes (e.g., stem base details)

LOCATION _____   **DATE** _____

_____

_____

GPS COORDINATES _____

WEATHER _____

HABITAT (Note where mushroom is sprouting—e.g., in disturbed soil, on decomposing log, at base of tree trunk—

and identify nearby trees and plants.) _____

_____

_____

_____

_____

PROBABLE SPECIES _____

CAP CHARACTERISTICS _____

    Color _____   Spore color _____

    Shape _____   Diameter _____

    Texture _____

    Condition _____

    Gills, teeth, pores, or other _____

    Additional notes (e.g., odor) _____

_____

_____

STEM CHARACTERISTICS _____

    Color _____   Height _____

    Shape _____   Diameter _____

    Texture _____

    Additional notes (e.g., stem base details) _____

_____

_____

_____

LOCATION   DATE

_____

_____

GPS COORDINATES
_____

WEATHER
_____

HABITAT (Note where mushroom is sprouting—e.g., in disturbed soil, on decomposing log, at base of tree trunk—

and identify nearby trees and plants.)

_____

_____

_____

_____

PROBABLE SPECIES
_____

CAP CHARACTERISTICS
_____

   Color   Spore color

   Shape   Diameter

   Texture

   Condition

   Gills, teeth, pores, or other

   Additional notes (e.g., odor)

_____

_____

STEM CHARACTERISTICS
_____

   Color   Height

   Shape   Diameter

   Texture

   Additional notes (e.g., stem base details)

_____

_____

_____

LOCATION

DATE

GPS COORDINATES

WEATHER

HABITAT (Note where mushroom is sprouting—e.g., in disturbed soil, on decomposing log, at base of tree trunk—and identify nearby trees and plants.)

PROBABLE SPECIES

CAP CHARACTERISTICS

Color   Spore color

Shape   Diameter

Texture

Condition

Gills, teeth, pores, or other

Additional notes (e.g., odor)

STEM CHARACTERISTICS

Color   Height

Shape   Diameter

Texture

Additional notes (e.g., stem base details)

LOCATION   DATE

_____

_____

GPS COORDINATES
_____

WEATHER
_____

HABITAT (Note where mushroom is sprouting—e.g., in disturbed soil, on decomposing log, at base of tree trunk—

and identify nearby trees and plants.)
_____

_____

_____

_____

PROBABLE SPECIES
_____

CAP CHARACTERISTICS

Color	Spore color
Shape	Diameter
Texture	
Condition	
Gills, teeth, pores, or other	
Additional notes (e.g., odor)	

_____

_____

STEM CHARACTERISTICS

Color	Height
Shape	Diameter
Texture	
Additional notes (e.g., stem base details)	

_____

_____

_____

LOCATION   DATE

GPS COORDINATES

WEATHER

HABITAT (Note where mushroom is sprouting—e.g., in disturbed soil, on decomposing log, at base of tree trunk—and identify nearby trees and plants.)

PROBABLE SPECIES

CAP CHARACTERISTICS

Color	Spore color
Shape	Diameter
Texture	
Condition	
Gills, teeth, pores, or other	
Additional notes (e.g., odor)	

STEM CHARACTERISTICS

Color	Height
Shape	Diameter
Texture	
Additional notes (e.g., stem base details)	

LOCATION _____ DATE _____

_____

_____

GPS COORDINATES _____

WEATHER _____

HABITAT (Note where mushroom is sprouting—e.g., in disturbed soil, on decomposing log, at base of tree trunk—

and identify nearby trees and plants.) _____

_____

_____

_____

_____

PROBABLE SPECIES _____

CAP CHARACTERISTICS _____

    Color _____ Spore color _____

    Shape _____ Diameter _____

    Texture _____

    Condition _____

    Gills, teeth, pores, or other _____

    Additional notes (e.g., odor) _____

_____

_____

STEM CHARACTERISTICS _____

    Color _____ Height _____

    Shape _____ Diameter _____

    Texture _____

    Additional notes (e.g., stem base details) _____

_____

_____

_____

LOCATION   **DATE**

GPS COORDINATES

WEATHER

HABITAT (Note where mushroom is sprouting—e.g., in disturbed soil, on decomposing log, at base of tree trunk—

and identify nearby trees and plants.)

PROBABLE SPECIES

CAP CHARACTERISTICS

Color   Spore color

Shape   Diameter

Texture

Condition

Gills, teeth, pores, or other

Additional notes (e.g., odor)

STEM CHARACTERISTICS

Color   Height

Shape   Diameter

Texture

Additional notes (e.g., stem base details)

LOCATION
DATE

GPS COORDINATES

WEATHER

HABITAT (Note where mushroom is sprouting—e.g., in disturbed soil, on decomposing log, at base of tree trunk— and identify nearby trees and plants.)

PROBABLE SPECIES

CAP CHARACTERISTICS

Color | Spore color

Shape | Diameter

Texture

Condition

Gills, teeth, pores, or other

Additional notes (e.g., odor)

STEM CHARACTERISTICS

Color | Height

Shape | Diameter

Texture

Additional notes (e.g., stem base details)

LOCATION   DATE

GPS COORDINATES

WEATHER

HABITAT (Note where mushroom is sprouting—e.g., in disturbed soil, on decomposing log, at base of tree trunk—
and identify nearby trees and plants.)

PROBABLE SPECIES

CAP CHARACTERISTICS

Color   Spore color

Shape   Diameter

Texture

Condition

Gills, teeth, pores, or other

Additional notes (e.g., odor)

STEM CHARACTERISTICS

Color   Height

Shape   Diameter

Texture

Additional notes (e.g., stem base details)

LOCATION

DATE

GPS COORDINATES

WEATHER

HABITAT (Note where mushroom is sprouting—e.g., in disturbed soil, on decomposing log, at base of tree trunk—
and identify nearby trees and plants.)

PROBABLE SPECIES

CAP CHARACTERISTICS

Color	Spore color
Shape	Diameter
Texture	
Condition	
Gills, teeth, pores, or other	
Additional notes (e.g., odor)	

STEM CHARACTERISTICS

Color	Height
Shape	Diameter
Texture	
Additional notes (e.g., stem base details)	

LOCATION   **DATE**

GPS COORDINATES

WEATHER

HABITAT (Note where mushroom is sprouting—e.g., in disturbed soil, on decomposing log, at base of tree trunk—and identify nearby trees and plants.)

PROBABLE SPECIES

CAP CHARACTERISTICS

Color	Spore color
Shape	Diameter
Texture	
Condition	
Gills, teeth, pores, or other	
Additional notes (e.g., odor)	

STEM CHARACTERISTICS

Color	Height
Shape	Diameter
Texture	
Additional notes (e.g., stem base details)	

MOUNTAINEERS BOOKS
Enjoy your foraging adventures. And remember to Leave No Trace, www.lnt.org

Copyright © 2022 Mountaineers Books

All rights reserved. No part of this book may be reproduced or utilized in any form, or by any electronic, mechanical, or other means, without the prior written permission of the publisher.

Printed in South Korea

Printed on FSC®-certified materials

ISBN 978-1-68051-633-3

An independent nonprofit publisher since 1960